© Cathy McGough 2022

Hardcover updated version published in September, 2025.

All Rights Reserved. No part of this publication may be reproduced or transmitted in any form or by any means, electronic or mechanical, including photocopy, recording or any other information storage and retrieval system, without prior permission in writing from the publisher at Stratford Living Publishing.

ISBN Print: 9781998651832

Cathy McGough has asserted her right under the Copyright, Designs and Patents Act, 1988 to be identified as the author of this work.

Art Powered by Canva Pro.

This is a work of fiction. The characters in it are all fiction. Resemblance to any persons living or dead is purely coincidental. Names, characters, places and incidents either are the products of the author's imagination or are used fictitiously.

Dedicated to Jenna

This is a book about looking for clues...

And being a detective or private eye...

To solve a mystery at my home...

When no one could solve it - I decided to give it a try!

First, I need to blend in, just like all famous detectives do...

And like them, I need tools to help me through!

1/ A super-powered flashlight for at night...

2/ A magnifying glass for zeroing in on hard to see clues.

3/ Powder and clear tape are necessary to get things right...

For lifting fingerprints left behind...

4/ Help from the local police...

To check out any prints I find.

And now it's time to Jump Jump Jump and Look For A Clue!

But first you need to know about the mystery...

Of things disappearing before our very eyes!

Mom asks, "Where's my jewellery gone?"

Dad says, "Hey, who's taken all my ties?!"

And all my sister does is cry...

Because she lost her badge for 1ˢᵗ prize!

And me, well, I lost some t-shirts and a gaming device!

Whoever is doing this, isn't very nice!

Just like Sherlock Holmes did...

Because he knew what to do!

I'm going to JUMP JUMP JUMP!

AND LOOK FOR A CLUE!

TASTE

TOUCH

SIGHT

HEARING

My super sniffer puppy will help me to...

JUMP, JUMP JUMP AND LOOK FOR A CLUE!

Clues can be hiding, or out in the open...

They may be easy or difficult to find!

They might even be right there in front of you!

That's why it's best to keep an open mind!

Sometimes the clues come looking for you!

It's like the clue wants to find you!

Then Arthur sniffs the air... he wags his tail and runs out the door!

I follow him, and it's true... my dog ARTHUR - IS THE CLUE!

And now it's time to Jump Jump Jump

Because we followed the clues!

JUMP SERIES:

Jump Like a Caribou!
Jump Like a Kangaroo!
Jump at the Zoo!
Jump and Say P.U.!
Jump and Say Boo!
Jump and Say Valentine's Day Is
For Kids Too!
Jump and Look For a Clue!
Jump and Say Happy Birthday to You!
Jump For Everything Blue!
Jump, Hop and Say Happy Easter To You!
Jump and Say Cock-A-Doodle-Do!
Jump and Sing Da-Do-Do-Do!
Jump and Ask Who? Who?
Jump and Squawk Like a Cockatoo!
Jump and Ask Is It You or Ewe?
Jump and Say There's an Ewww in My Stew!
Jump and Say Merry Christmas To You!
Jump and Cheer Happy New Year!
Jump and Say There's a Moo-Moo in a Tutu!
Jump and Say There's a Hare in My Hair!
Jump and Say My Aunt Ate An Ant!
Jump and Say There's An Aardvark
In The Amusement Park!
Jump and Roar For The Dinosaurs!
Jump and Buzz Like A Bee!
Jump and Flutter Like A Butterfly!
Jump and Pop Like Popcorn!
Jump and Ribbit Like A Frog!
Jump and Snore Like A Koala!
Jump and Snuffle Like A Platypus!
Jump and Grunt Like A Groundhog!

Jump and Say Hello!
Jump and Say Friend!
Jump and Say Peace!
Jump and Say Sky!
Jump and Say Merry Christmas!
Jump and Say Happy New Year!
Jump and Say Fun!
Jump and Say Family!
Jump and Say Jump!

CLAP FOR SERIES:
Clap for 1!
Clap for 2!
Clap for 3!
Clap for 4!
Clap for 5!
Clap for 6!
Clap for 7!
Clap for 8!
Clap for 9!
Clap for 10!

The Cat Who Said Hello
The Three Boulders
Billy Shakespeare
Billie Shakespeare
Learn To Draw With Symmetry
ABC More Learn to Draw With Symmetry

POETRY SERIES:
There's a Chimpanzee Inside of Me!

Non-Fiction
103 Fundraising Ideas For Parent Volunteers With Schools and Teams

www.ingramcontent.com/pod-product-compliance
Lightning Source LLC
Chambersburg PA
CBHW041455010526
44107CB00014B/1046